A Small B.I.B.L.E. of Biblical Acronyms

Heaven's Refreshing Well-Springs of Wisdom and Knowledge

Also included are
Short Poems
and
Proverbial Quotes

Harold L. Sweet

The Lord giveth wisdom: out of His mouth cometh knowledge and understanding. (Proverbs 2:6)

EVP

Earthen Vessel Publishing

A Small B.I.B.L.E. of Biblical Acronyms

©Copyright 2013 Harold L. Sweet

ISBN 978-0-9907277-9-8

Published 2015, 2020
Earthen Vessel Publishing
San Rafael, CA

Edited by Stephanie Adams
Book design by Katie L. C. Philpott
Cover design by Dammeion Butler

Unless otherwise noted, all Scripture quotations are taken from the King James version of the Bible.

All rights reserved. No part of this publication may be reproduced, distributed, or transmitted in any form or by any means, or stored in a database or retrieval system, without the prior permission of the author.

For author's permission, email:
HLSweetBibleAcronyms@gmail.com

Personal Praise for
A Small B.I.B.L.E. of Biblical Acronyms

"Whether you are a seeker, new believer, or seasoned saint; as you lay hold of this book, it will lay hold of you. Author Harold L. Sweet is absolutely brilliant in stating simple, concise, profound truths through scriptures, poems, and acronyms, which are easily remembered.

His acronymic style of teaching will bring you more insight and understanding of scriptures and of key words used repetitively throughout the Bible, while adding a new freshness and fun into studying.

Surely, this book will move you to take up your 'spiritual shovel,' as the Spirit takes you on a treasure hunt in search of nuggets of truth placed between each letter of key words of God."

Behold, I will do a new thing, now it shall spring forth.
Shall you not know it…? (Isaiah 43:19)

"Yes, Glory be to God, you're reading it!"

—Robert Adger, Ambassador of Christ

"Harold L. Sweet has combined the gift of creating dynamic acronyms with sound biblical doctrine to produce a work of art and inspiration. He is blessed with the ability to interpret Scriptures and make it come alive in this heartfelt work.

Every acronym gives special emphasis and meaning, and is a fitting ending to each of his commentaries. The collection of short poems and proverbial quotes are an added blessing to readers. This book is a must read for believers and non-believers alike."

—Larry M. Carter, Sr., Pastor/Evangelist

"A SMALL B.I.B.L.E. OF BIBLICAL ACRONYMS is surprisingly pleasant, spiritually uplifting, and a joy to read."
—Marylou Pettaway
Office Assistant III, Social Services
Crescent City, CA

"Every now and then, some little thing turns into a life-changing event. Who knows? One of Harold Sweet's acronyms, together with the devotional thought or poem he puts with it, may become a turning point in your life. But it can't happen unless you read them!"
—Marvin Moore

"A SMALL B.I.B.L.E. OF BIBLICAL ACRONYMS combines scriptures with inspirational insight and comfort to the reader. I encourage every reader to prayerfully take in the wealth of this thought-provoking collection of ideas. A great blessing will be yours."
—Dr. Joel O. Martin, DD, MA

SPECIAL DEDICATION

This book is dedicated to Maria Benak, that heaven sent spark of inspiration that joyously ignited the spiritual passion of my incarcerated soul to write this book. Thank you! Maria, you were a God-send!

Contents

AUTHOR'S PREFACE	10
B.I.B.L.E.	12
G.O.S.P.E.L.	14
F.A.I.T.H.	16
J.E.S.U.S.	19
P.O.E.M.	21
P.R.A.Y.	22
P.R.A.Y.E.R.	24
S.W.O.R.D.	26
G.R.A.C.E.	28
C.H.U.R.C.H.	30
V.I.C.T.O.R.S.	32
D.O.O.R.	34
T.R.U.T.H. - 1	36
T.R.U.T.H. - 2	38
A.W.O.K.E.	41
W.A.R. - 1	44
W.A.R. - 2	46

H.O.M.E.	49
H.O.P.E.	52
J.O.Y.	54
P.O.P.E.	55
Proverbial Quotations	59
Poetry Selections	65
Preview of Volume 2: L.O.G.O.S.	72
Preview of Volume 2: Who Am I?	77
About the Author	78

Author's Preface

Noah Webster defines the word "acronym" as: a word formed from the initial letter or letters of each of the successive parts or major parts of a compound term. Now, I admit that until not too long ago, I never had any idea whatsoever what an acronym was.

The first time I came to know of its meaning was when a Christian inmate informed me that the word B.I.B.L.E. stood for Basic Instruction Before Leaving Earth. This is probably the most famous and widely known and used Biblical acronym by preachers, teachers, and Christian believers today. But in any case, I thought that the particular acronym for B.I.B.L.E. was no more than a simple one-time creative shot in the scriptural dark, which 'just so happened' to fit the overall spiritual meaning of the word. Surely then, I thought, there couldn't be anymore scripturally relevant ones.

That is, until one day I was sharing one of my poems with another Christian inmate, who asked me, "Do you know what the G.O.S.P.E.L. stands for?" I replied, "No, what?" He told me it means God's Only Son Preached Everlasting Life! Wow, I just stood there with my mouth wide open. But then immediately a flood of creative fire instantly began to fill my heart and mind, causing me to run back to my prison cell, where the Holy Spirit came upon me and wonderfully caused me to write a poem using the acronyms for both the BIBLE as well as for the GOSPEL.

They're included in this book.

However, I was forever changed by these spiritually creative, biblically profound and thought-provoking acronyms. Therefore, I wanted more! But, were there any more acronyms to be found in the Bible? So, I was armed only with the single willingness to know; then by faith, I was led by the divine Guide and Teacher, the Holy Spirit, for He alone pointed the way.

Then I eagerly set out upon a search of the Bible, to see and discover for myself whether there were other spiritually profound and relevant 'acronymic streams' of wisdom and knowledge, flowing unseen just beneath and between the scriptural surfaces and sacred spaces of God's immutable word. And to my very delightful surprise then, the Spirit of God would in no wise disappoint. For He did surely lead me to a small yet strong stream of hidden acronyms, just silently flowing there through the Bible for two thousand years, just waiting to be discovered—until now!

So, this little book is a direct result of that particular diligent search, and of its joyous findings. It is my blessed hope that you will take the time out of your daily, and no doubt, sometimes weary routine travelings to inquisitively draw from its cooling springs that your spiritually parched souls might be 'replenished and refreshed' within the full saving knowledge of the Gospel of Jesus Christ and of His soon coming glory!

Also, I've included for your spiritual enjoyment other proverbial quotes, short Christian poems, and profound sayings. I hope you will come to enjoy this little book that has been put together just for you! May God greatly bless you as you seek to become more acquainted with His Word.

Harold L. Sweet
Maranatha!

Acronym One

Study to shew thyself approved unto God, a workman that needeth not to be ashamed, rightly dividing the word of truth.... But continue thou in the things which thou hast learned and hast been assured of, knowing of whom thou hast learned them; And that from a child thou hast known the holy scriptures, which are able to make thee wise unto salvation through faith which is in Christ Jesus. All scripture is given by inspiration of God, and is profitable for doctrine, for reproof, for correction, for instruction in righteousness: That the man of God may be perfect, throughly furnished unto all good works. (2 Timothy 2:15; 3:14-17)

When was the last time you read that book on your shelf, the one with the dust all over its face? Oh, don't be so naïve, you know which one — the one that speaks of God's love and saving grace!

Well, since you're slow to answer me by now, then I take it you haven't read its sacred pages in quite some time. What? You consider it to be a book of useless knowledge? Oh, you impatient, simple mind. Know you not that if you would simply endure your studies, the blessings of God's true wisdom you will find?

Do not fail to further read it as a result of the spiritual-ridicule this poem has to say. Because it's only yourself, towards those cherry wood shelves, that you stack God's good book away, holding within your erroneous mind, "Every now and then, I'll just simply pray!"

Do not be so deceived, for the closing times of our final salvation is surely near. Thus, from the very first moment of our earthly births, God intended for us to read our

Basic **I**nstructions **B**efore **L**eaving **E**arth!

Acronym Two

In the fullness of time, God sent His Son into the world
To recreate us within the likeness of His face.
He came that we might have life more abundantly
So that we, as forgiven sinners,
Might show forth the light of His esteeming grace.

He came into the world, and the world was made by Him,
But the world counted His birth an unknown thing.
Yet, sweet cherubs above, attending shepherds,
Did hail their Creator, and "Glory be to God in the Highest,"
Is what they did joyfully sing!

As a young child, He grew up among His Jewish own;
Yet as a man, He was despised and rejected by all His kin.
But still, He chose to be acquainted with all their grief;
He bore their sorrows; His mind knew no wrong;
His heart, no sin.

John bore witness that the Word was the light of the world.
So John dared to touch the feet of Him
Who treads the mighty seas.
But that Word bade him, "Baptize me, John."
The Spirit descended as a dove, and the heavens spoke,
"This is My beloved son, in whom I am well pleased!"

He was tempted in all points just like you and I.
Thus, into the wilderness of temptation He did spiritedly go!
With "Get behind Me, Satan," did He assail that subtle tempter,
So that the power of His word, He might clearly show!

He gave sight unto the blind, and speech unto the dumb.
And with the same finger of God,
Out of possessed souls, did demons cry.
"Come forth Lazarus," and he who was dead did awake!
And glory was given to God by those who were standing by.

He went into the streets not to speak any trumpet-like fame,
Just to receive unnecessary attention from watching men.
He came to magnify the law. He made it honorable.
He set judgment in the earth. He came to die
For our iniquities, and rise again!

Now there are also many other things
That Jesus said and did
That were not written down within this old world
Of sin and strife.
But these things are written,
So that you might believe that

God's **O**nly **S**on **P**reached **E**verlasting **L**ife

Acronym Three

But without faith it is impossible to please him: for he that cometh to God must believe that he is, and that he is a rewarder of them that diligently seek him. (Hebrews 11:6)

Four times, God declares that if He should send famine, pestilence, sword, or noisome beast throughout the land to destroy it, "Even if Noah, Daniel and Job were in it, ... they would save only themselves by their righteousness saith the Lord God" (Ezekiel 14:12–20).

What's so important and special about these three men that God should hold them in such high regard? Well, it had to do with their faith in God! Each one had exercised a different level of faith within their personal relationships with Him, which caused them to greatly trust God with their very lives—lives that would be thoroughly tested and severely tried to the utmost!

First would be Noah, who was obedient and righteous in faith. By faith, Noah, being warned of God of things not seen as yet, moved with fear, prepared an ark to the saving of his house...thereby proving himself righteous, in that, he went about preaching righteousness unto the sinful antediluvians of his time, that they should repent and get in the boat! But we all know the sad outcome of the story (Hebrews 11:6; II Peter 2:5).

In any case, Noah not only believed the warning of God that He would destroy the world, but he also trusted God's ability and willingness to save him and his entire family. As a result of such well-placed trust, God greatly blessed him!

Next, we have the well-beloved Daniel, who was courageous and wise in faith. By faith, Daniel had refused to eat the portion of the king's meat, and God blessed him as a direct result, by making his countenance appear fairer and fatter in flesh than all the children who did eat the portion of the king's meat (Daniel 1:9–16). Later on, by faith, Daniel calmly stayed the hand of Babylon's executioner, Arioch, the captain of the king's guard, by greeting him with "counsel and wisdom" (Daniel 2:13–14). By faith, Daniel had the courage and boldness to walk into the presence of the angry king in order to ask him for time in which to interpret his dream, trusting that God would reveal it to him, which He did (Daniel 2:17–23).

And lastly, by the same courageously bold faith, Daniel still prayed when he knew that Darius' decree to throw him into the lions' den had been signed. Yet God showed up for him that night and shut the mouths of the lions, all because Daniel trusted in God! (Daniel 6:6–8).

And then we have Job, who was patient and steadfast in faith. By faith, Job patiently endured the destruction of all his wealth, property and children all in one day. Yet still, in all of this, Job sinned not, nor charged God foolishly (Job 1:1–22). Afterwards, when the devil saw that Job was not moved by such adverse circumstances, he descended a second time with a "boil-tipped" finger and severely smote Job from foot to crown. But still, Job held fast to his integrity and refused to curse God, but chose to bless Him with his lips instead (Job 2:1–10).

Now, we don't know how long Job was allowed to suffer in his afflicted state, but however long it was, by faith, Job was steadfast in his love, loyalty and allegiance to God. And still, despite the miserable "comforting" and accusations of his three friends, Job would determine to endure his plight, saying,

"Though He [God] slay me, yet will I trust Him...but He [God] knoweth the way that I take; when He has tried me, I shall come forth as gold" (Job 13:15; 23:10).

At the end of Job's ordeal, we find God blessing him with sevenfold more substance and children than he had before, all because Job trusted God to bring him through, which He did (Job 2:10–17; James 5:11).

So, if you want to please God like Noah, Daniel and Job, then, just like them, you must have

Firm Assurance In Trusting Him!

Acronym Four

"And she shall bring forth a son, and thou shalt call his name JESUS: for he shall save his people from their sins." (Matthew 1:21)

So declared the angel Gabriel unto the Virgin Mary. But what's so particularly special about the name of Jesus? It universally reveals God's free-willingness to both love and redeem sinful mankind.

How so? The Hebrew word for Jesus is YESHUA, which means "Jehovah saves." So every time we say the name of Jesus, we're faithfully making a divine statement of fact. However, it should be rightly noted that according to the actual meaning of His name, Jesus never saves anyone. But rather, it is Jehovah (God the Father) through Jesus' faithful and obedient actions, that He is both able and willing to save us lost sinners.

The Bible further clearly confirms this when the Apostle Paul declares unto the young Timothy that "Without controversy, great is the mystery of godliness. God was manifest in the flesh, justified in the Spirit, seen of angels, preached unto the Gentiles, believed on in the world, received up into glory" (1 Timothy 3:16).

No wonder then, that in preparing for Himself a body to inhabit, God also specially prepared and selected for Himself a particular name—one that, along with the eternal wounds of his crucified and gloriously resurrected body would adequately express and spontaneously bring to redeemed minds all that He alone has done for them at Calvary.

A name that would reveal His mighty deity as God, while at the same time, His humble humanity as man; a name that serves as a perpetual memorial of His unfathomable love; a name that would be above every other name that is named—both in this world as well as the one to come.

An excellent name I say—that in the end, when all is finally said and done, will harmoniously cause every knee to bow and every tongue to confess who Jesus Christ really was, is, and evermore will be.

So, the next time someone asks you the question, "How are we saved?", just tell them, "Through God's Only Begotten Son

Jehovah **E**ternally **S**aves **U**s **S**inners"

Acronym Five

For we are his workmanship, created in Christ Jesus unto good works, which God hath before ordained that we should walk in them. (Ephesians 2:10)

A poem or poetry is rightly defined as anything that didn't exist before, but was created from the imagination of a person's mind, and then fixed in permanent form.

Thus, all of creation is poetry! All living things, both great and small, seen and unseen, spontaneously ushered forth from the creative imagination of God's unfathomable mind, being forever fixed by the Word of His power, within the permanent form of what we call earthly reality (Psalms 33:8–9; Romans 1:20).

However, the greatest of all created epic poems that the Mastermind of the universe did ever imagine and bring forth into existence, was that of mankind! In the above verse of Ephesians, the word "workmanship" is translated from the Greek word *poiema*, from which we get our English word "poem."

So you see, God is indeed a Poet! Thus, we who do believe in Him by faith are His

— lovingly created in Jesus Christ!

Acronym Six

And when thou prayest, thou shalt not be as the hypocrites are: for they love to pray standing in the synagogues and in the corners of the streets, that they may be seen of men. Verily I say unto you, They have their reward. But thou, when thou prayest, enter into thy closet, and when thou hast shut thy door, pray to thy Father which is in secret; and thy Father which seeth in secret shall reward thee openly. But when ye pray, use not vain repetitions, as the heathen do: for they think that they shall be heard for their much speaking. Be not ye therefore like unto them: for your Father knoweth what things ye have need of, before ye ask him. After this manner therefore pray ye:

"Our Father in heaven, hallowed be your name.
Your kingdom come, your will be done,
on earth as it is in heaven.
Give us this day our daily bread,
and forgive us our debts,
as we also have forgiven our debtors.
And lead us not into temptation,
but deliver us from evil."
For thine is the kingdom, and the power, and the glory, for ever.
Amen.
(Matthew 6:5-13)

*T*here was perhaps one thing that Jesus did more than anything else while here on earth to which His disciples gave very close attentive notice; Jesus always found time to pray.

No doubt, there were even times when Jesus' disciples may have done a little eaves-dropping on some of His private time with His heavenly Father, when they would hear him praying more for them, the welfare of lost sinners, the things of the Kingdom of Heaven, the forgiveness of His enemies, and for those things that overall pleased God rather than Himself.

To the disciples' surprise, this type of caring and compassionate speech wasn't the kind of praying they were used to hearing or were familiar with, because the high and self-mighty religious leaders of their day had taught that unless a person was learned and eloquent in communicating with heaven, as the Jewish High-Priest, who ministers amid the swirling sweet-incense and peculiar odors within the temple, or unless one had the capacity to remember and recite the long prayerful stanzas of the proverbial words and songs of David's Psalms, their prayers would not and could not be effectively heard or answered. So Jesus' disciples came to Him at an opportune time in order to gain a better understanding about the proper and effective prayer. They asked, "Lord, teach us how to pray."

Jesus then proceeded to teach His disciples in essence that when we pray, we are to speak to God, our heavenly Father, with the simplicity of a young child, using only those genuine words that are within the sincere innocence of a yielding heart, as we would speak to our parents and humbly communicate to them all our desires, while at the same time, keeping in mind all those things that they themselves would desire of us.

This particular humble and contrite spirit God will in no wise despise, but bend His ear near to hear and answer. Therefore, always remember that in reciting the Lord's Prayer, Jesus was not teaching His disciples what to say, but how to:

Personally **R**each **A**donai **Y**ehovah!

Acronym Seven

P.R.A.Y.E.R.

Then said he unto me, "Fear not, Daniel: for from the first day that thou didst set thine heart to understand, and to chasten thyself before thy God, thy words were heard, and I am come for thy words." (Daniel 10:12)

Praise waiteth for thee, O God, in Sion: And unto thee shall the vow be performed. O thou that hearest prayer, Unto thee shall all flesh come. (Psalm 65:1-2)

The sacrifice of the wicked is an abomination to the Lord: But the prayer of the upright is his delight. (Proverbs 15:8)

God is a God who loves to hear the prayers of His saints. From the very first moment we bend our knees and bow our heads to speak and present them, He hears them! Surely nobody knew this better than Daniel, the beloved prophet of God.

Daniel considered prayer to be the golden cord of blessed communication between himself and heaven. He had always received a prompt and speedy answer, even in some very dire times and situations. No matter what Daniel might be faced with, he always trusted that God would hear and answer his prayers.

Yet there was this one time, when Daniel hadn't received an answer to his prayer for three full weeks; he knew something was amiss; it wasn't like God to have him wait! Daniel began to fast, putting himself into a holding pattern, until the angel Gabriel was able to break through the demonic opposition that sought to prevent Daniel from receiving God's answer.

A holding pattern can be thought of as occurring when a child of God chooses to hold onto and trust the promises of God, maintaining a steadfast faith despite the seeming delays, that He has already granted his or her petition from the moment it was spoken.

So if you've been waiting for some time now for the answers to your prayers, it could be that your angel is fighting for you. So until he arrives with answer in hand, place yourself in a holding pattern of trust, for you too are greatly beloved of God, just like Daniel.

So praise God and glorify Him for the answer. And keep giving Him praise and glory until it arrives! For there is one thing that will never know any delay—the earnest words of your mouth.

Personally

Reach

Adonai

Yehovah's

Ears

Right-away

Acronym Eight

And take the helmet of salvation, and the sword of the Spirit, which is the word of God. (Ephesians 6:17)

The Bible says that immediately after Jesus was baptized by John the Baptist at the river Jordan, the Spirit drove (led) Him into the wilderness to be tempted of Satan.

However, the Holy Spirit would not have done this unless He had first taught Jesus how to effectively fight and overcome such a mighty and cunning opponent, the requisite skill and knowledge being obtained only by reading and obediently acting accordingly with the written word of God.

Obviously, the Holy Spirit had started extremely early in educating and preparing Jesus for his upcoming title-bout for this world with Satan in the wilderness. After all, at the tender age of twelve, Jesus was said to have been in the Jewish temple for three days sitting in the midst of the doctors, both hearing them and asking them questions (Luke 2:46).

Jesus must have taken the time daily to acquaint Himself with the word of God, which at that time consisted only of the law, (the first five books of the Bible), the Prophets and the Psalms—these being the three sections of the Old Testament Scripture that Jesus used to overcome the fiery darts of Satan's subtle temptations.

Jesus readily possessed a spiritually righteous defense for

every temptation that Satan hurled at Him by simply deflecting them with the famous words, "It is written," implying that regarding each offer of Satan, Jesus knew what the Bible said about it, where it was found in the Bible and what it meant. And against such faithful and obedient knowledge and self-determined quotation of scripture, the devil had no power that could be used to advance against Christ.

Therefore, neither against you my friend, can he!

So the word of the Lord is not just our Basic Instruction Before Leaving Earth, but it is also intended to be our:

Spiritual **W**eapon **O**f **R**ighteous **D**efense

Acronym Nine

For the grace of God that bringeth salvation hath appeared to all men. (Titus 2:11)

Grace is spiritually defined as "unmerited divine assistance" and is given to man for his sanctification and regeneration. The particular divine assistance that we as sinners freely received from God, and didn't deserve, first came down to us within the gifted form of Jesus Christ (John 4:10), who was and is the "Grace of God" that Immanuelly-appeared in order to bring the knowledge unto mankind by teaching them through his daily example of how to live the victorious life in which God beforehand preordained for all men to righteously live (Titus 2:11–14).

Now, upon the earthly completion of his redemptive work and his return to heaven, Jesus sent back down unto us within his substituted place the gifted form of the Holy Spirit (Acts 2:38), who was and is the grace of God that would invisibly appear in order to sanctify and empower us to daily live the life of victory, which Christ taught us to live by faith in God (John 16:5–15).

So you see, both Jesus and the Holy Spirit are said to be "The Gift of God" and "The Grace of God." That's because by the personal work and ministry of both are we saved!

Both are our comforter (advocate) (John 14:1618; 1 John

2:12).

Both are our Intercessor (Hebrews 7:25; Romans 8:26–27).

Both purchased the Church of God with their own blood (Acts 20:28).

Both are our teachers (Matthew 23:8; Colossians 43:1; John 14:26).

Both are the truth (John 14:6;16:13).

So there were and are no self-righteous works that we have done, or ever can do that would be adequate and sufficient to procure all the wonderful blessings of heaven's divine-assistance, that we today are enjoying daily and using for our eternal benefit! We can only thank God by freely believing in His Son (John 1:7), and accepting His Spirit (John 3:24).

Yet, as in giving any kind of gift, it needs to be BOUGHT first! Not by the receiver, but by the giver.

Therefore, eternal life is by no means free; it cost God the death of His Son. Thus it is by God's

Gift **R**eceived **A**t **C**hrist's **E**xpense

that we are saved!

Acronym Ten

C.H.U.R.C.H.

"...And upon this rock I will build my church and the gates of hell shall not prevail against it." (Matthew 16:18)

The Greek word for church is *ecclesia* and it means "those who are called out." So the church is not a particular building in which we gather for weekly worship services; nor is it a particular denomination of which we have been a part.

The church is a particular people, regardless of race, whom the Holy Spirit calls out of the world in order that He might wash them from the filth of their sins and freely give them a clean change of garments. After sanctifying, consecrating and empowering them to go back out into the same sinful world from whence they have emerged, they might be both light and salt unto those who, like themselves, were lost in darkness and without the savior of life in their lives, Jesus Christ (1 Peter 2:9).

Those who are called out...

...belong to Christ. They are His property, because they were bought with a price (I Corinthians 6:19–20); and that high price was the BLOOD of Jesus (Acts 20:28).

Those who are called out...

...are to be holy, even as God in heaven is holy (Ephesians 2:24; 1 Thessalonians 3:13; Hebrews 12:14).

Those who are called out...

...are unified. This was and is Jesus' specific will and prayer to His heavenly Father. Jesus prayed that "they may be one, as we are" (John 17:11; Ephesians 4:3; Galatians 3:28).

Those who are called out...

...are to be righteous even as Jesus is righteous.

Those who are called out...

...are God's building (1 Corinthians 3:9). It is by His loving power to save them through Jesus that He is able to rebuild them in His original likeness and image. They are being prepared for their eternal abode.

Those who are called out...

...are to become a habitation in which God the Father, God the Son, and God the Holy Spirit might forever live and abide (Ephesians 1:19–22).

So, always remember that God has called us out of the world to be:

Christ's

Holy

Unified

Righteously

Constructed

Habitation

Acronym Eleven

Thine, O Lord, is the greatness, and the power, and the glory, and the victory. (I Chronicles 29:11)

As new believers in Christ, we are expected to overcome. Seven times in the book of Revelation, Jesus admonishes and encourages the churches of all ages by saying, "He that overcometh..." (Revelation 2:7,11,17,26) and then goes on to promise an eternal reward to all those who manage by faith and patience to do so!

But what are we to overcome? Well, the beloved disciple, John, says that it's not the physical world around us, but rather "according to the course of the spiritual world, according to the prince of the power of the air, the spirit that now worketh in the children of disobedience" (Ephesians 2:2). This particular world is said to be in our natures. John describes it as the lust of the flesh, the lust of the eyes and the pride of life. This is the battle that every Christian must wage daily, and ultimately overcome if they are to be victorious!

How can we be victorious? Once again, John declares, "And this is the victory that overcometh the world, even our faith" (1 John 5:4); and that faith must be in Jesus, who said that "I have overcome the world" (John 16:33).

So if we are to make peace with God, we must make war with sin. There is no other way; we must overcome the sin that is in our old natures by daily choosing to live victoriously by the power of God's indwelling Spirit.

Furthermore, this victory over sin is also obtained by believing in the promises of God's word and having a steadfast willingness to abide within His word and his promises, some of which are:

"Nay, in all these things we are more than conquerors through him that loved us" (Romans 8:37).

"I can do all things through Christ who strengtheneth me" (Philippians 4:13).

"Because greater is he that is in you than he who is in the world" (1 John 4:4).

"Now unto him who is able to keep you from falling, and to present you faultless before the presence of his glory" (Jude 24).

There are many more promises concerning our victories in Christ, but time would not permit me to tell you about them all.

So, within our battle with sin, by faith in Jesus, heaven expects us to be

Valiant

In

Conquering

Through

Our

Redeeming

Savior

Acronym Twelve

"I am the door; by me if any man enter in, he shall be saved, and shall go in and out, and find pasture." (John 10:9)

Eli, the ancient priest of Israel, in sharply rebuking his two sons, Phinehas and Hophni, for wickedness, asked them the haunting question, "If a man sin against the Lord, who will entreat for him?" (Samuel 2:25).

Now, concerning our inherited natures as 'born sinners,' this character defect disqualifies us from entreating the Lord on our own behalf for the many iniquities and transgressions that we have committed against Him. For none of us, says the sweet psalmist, David, can by any means redeem our brothers or ourselves, nor ascend to heaven, even if it were possible, in order to present a ransom to God for ourselves or them. The redemption purchase of our sinful souls is too high and precious (Psalms 49:7–8).

It would therefore appear that our miserable cases of being forever guilty sinners is hopeless. Not so fast. In steps, a loving and compassionate God, who is all in all and knows all, has already foreknown before the foundation of the world that we wouldn't be able to redeem ourselves out of the sinful, chaotic mess that Adam's transgressional love for Eve had placed us all in.

He freely decided, while we were yet sinners, to appoint for us a 'DAYSMAN.' A daysman is one who is selected by the ruling courts to step in and represent the accused offender who is not able to supply or procure proper defense or legal representation for himself.

The job of the daysman is to argue, plead, justify, speak for, mediate, vindicate, and ultimately clear the accused of all charges, therefore setting him free! However, within our heavenly cases, the daysman was to be a "Lamb without blemish," who had to die so its precious blood might overflowingly be spilled! (1 Peter 1:18-21).

A daysman, who like us could sympathize with the feeling of our infirmities, was made like us in the flesh. He would be tempted like us in all points, yet without sin. This daysman was both graciously willing and mightily able to do for us what was impossible for us to do ourselves.

A daysman, I say, who would be willing to speak to God on our behalf whenever we may happen, through the weakness of our flesh, to fall into sin. That wonderful daysman is Jesus Christ.

Having paid the price for our redemption, He ascended on high into His Father's presence. There He now gloriously sits with His blood, applying and buying the eternal salvation of all who come to the Father through Him by faith and obedience.

Yes, as a direct result of what He was able to triumphantly accomplish at Calvary and is presently mercifully doing for us within the Holy of Holies as our great High Priest, we now have free access into the presence of God the Father, through Jesus Christ, the

Daysman Of Our Redemption!

Acronym Thirteen

"To wit, that God was in Christ, reconciling the world unto himself." (1 Corinthians 5:19)

Since the very beginning of the great controversy between God and Satan, Satan had brought the God of the universe upon charges of misconduct.

The justice of Heaven patiently allowed Satan to self-address the courts by saying that God's order of the banishment of Satan and his angels was both unfair and unreasonable. And, furthermore, it was totally contradictory to the image of Him as a loving and compassionate God.

Therefore, God's character as "merciful and gracious, long-suffering and abundant in goodness and truth" (Exodus 34:6) was being placed on trial before the entire universe, and being brought into evil refute by Satan.

In mounting a credible and successful defense against such false allegations, God couldn't use the testimony of his angels, because it would have represented a conflict of interest. Furthermore, for every angel that He could have called as a witness of His goodness, Satan could have called a hundred, a thousand, even a million of his angels to testify otherwise.

The only defense that God seemed to have against the accusation of Satan was himself. In the fullness of time, God was summoned down to honorably take the witness stand of this earth in the form of Jesus, in order to become a steadfast and faithful witness (Revelation 1:5) against Satan and his criminal lies which he has been perpetrating against God and His saints for over four thousand years.

All through Jesus Christ's earthly ministry, from the temptation in the wilderness to the last temptation in the garden of Gethsemane, Satan was permitted to cross-examine the Creator of the heavens in the hopes of entrapping Him into contradictions of His qualities of love and compassion (qualities which He had been exhibiting since the dawn of time). When Satan repeatedly failed in his attempt to get Jesus to sin, Satan lost it. In a fit of rage, he violently badgered the witness by inciting the Jewish leaders to arrest, falsely judge, and kill the Lord of all Glory. Satan did not understand that in so doing, he was forever sealing his doom (1 Corinthians 2:7–8).

In any case, Satan's actions against Christ proved to the heavenly courts that Satan was a thief, robber, murderer, and a liar. As a direct result, the high court of heaven had Satan held in contempt and forever cast down from heaven, from which there is no court of appeals (Luke 10:18; Revelations 12:10). Later, Satan is to be summoned back into their ruling presence to be judged (1 Corinthians 6:3), condemned and destroyed forever (Ezekiel 28:18–19; Malachi 4:1–3; Revelation 20:10).

As for God Himself — well, He had to wait for three days and three nights in order for heaven to deliberate the witnessing testimony of His Son Jesus and all that He bore for His honor and glory, and for mankind's redemption.

It was on the third day, early in the morning, when heaven reached a unanimous decision. The light of heaven's court room above swung open and sent down a glorious angel to summon forth from the grave the Son of God in order to deliver unto Him heaven's irrefutable verdict:

GOD WAS IN CHRIST
Triumphantly **R**econciling **U**s **T**o **H**imself!

Acronym Fourteen

Jesus saith unto him, "I am the way, the truth and the life; no man cometh unto the Father but by Me." (John14:6)

Truth: "Fidelity, consistency, sincerity of actions, character, and utterances; being faithful to the original or standard." So says Noah Webster.

Truth is rightly defined as being someone, not something, who is faithfully consistent and sincere within their actions, character, and conversations without having made an error of some kind within doing either.

There has been no one within the entire history of mankind who has been more faithfully consistent and sincere without ever faltering within their actions, character, and conversation but Jesus. Not Mohammed, not Gandhi, not Krishna, not Confucius, not the Dalai Lama, but Jesus.

So the only way to heaven has been consecrated by the bold footprints of Christ Jesus, and it is only by following his way that we, with joy, shall see God. That is the truth of the matter. Therefore, despite what is said today of the world's different religions—that one is just as good as the other, and that all roads lead to the selfsame God in heaven—it is a lie.

The Bible, being the sole authority as to the truth that is in Jesus Christ, states concerning the faithful consistency of his actions that even from a young child he himself said, "Know ye not, I must be about my Father's business" (Luke 2:49). Even from that time until his manhood, then it's said of him that "He increased in wisdom and favor with God and man" (Luke 2:52).

As a man, He continued to faithfully follow the pattern of obedience that he had exercised daily as a child "and went about doing good and healing all of those who were oppressed of the devil" (Acts 10:3). He said of himself that "I always do those things that please him" (John 8:29).

Concerning his character, the Bible says that it is the express image (exact copy) of God's person (Hebrews 1:3). It is also declared of Him that "He was without spot or blemish, and that he was without sin" (Hebrews 4:15; 1 Peter 1:19).

As for the utterances of his mouth it says that "There was found no guile nor deceit in his mouth" (Isaiah 53:9; 1 Peter 2:22). Even his enemies said of him "Never man spake like this man" (John 7:46).

You see, there was no fault in Jesus anywhere. Because He was truly successfully able to do all this while on earth could mean only one thing: He was and is the God of Truth, who is without iniquity (Deuteronomy 32:4), the spirit of truth who leads and guides (John 16:13), and the word of truth, who teaches and sanctifies (John 1:1-2; 3:31-32; 1 John 3:9; Psalms 119:11).

This is why Jesus authoritatively declared that He is the way we are to walk (1 John 2:6; 1 Peter 2:21), the truth we are to obey (Hebrews 5:9), and the life we are to live (John 6:54-57).

Nearing the end of his earthly ministry, knowing that He was indeed faithfully consistent in his heavenly Father's standard of righteousness and overall divine plan in restoring sinful mankind back unto Himself, He lifted up His eyes toward heaven and prayed, "I have glorified thee on earth; I have finished the work which thou gavest me to do" (John 17:4).

Thus, just a little while later, in condemning him to death, Herod and Pontius Pilate, with the Gentiles and the people of Israel, came to prove my expatiated point, that:

JESUS CHRIST IS THE

Triumphant **R**edeemer **U**nder **T**he **H**eavens!

Acronym Fifteen

A.W.O.K.E.

"Watch ye therefore, for ye know not when the master of the house cometh; at even, or at the cockcrowing, or in the morning, lest coming suddenly he find you sleeping." (Mark 13:35-36)

To the King of the ages, immortal, invisible, the only God, be honor and glory forever and ever. Amen. (1 Timothy 1:17)

Blessed is that servant whom his master will find so doing when he comes. Truly, I say to you, he will set him over all his possessions. (Matthew 24:46–47)

In telling the parable of the Ten Pounds (Luke 19:11–26), Jesus was prophetically laying out before His disciples all that He would expect from them as well as every believer, from the time of His ascension to heaven, until the time of His second coming back to this earth.

As the parable goes, the nobleman who was about to go to a far country to receive for himself a kingdom and to return represents Jesus Christ, who ascended to the far away country of heaven in order to receive from His Father "dominion, and glory, and a kingdom" (Hebrews 11:6; Daniel 7:13–14).

Right before the nobleman takes his trip, he turns to the servants whom he has selected to serve him in his long absence, and commands them," Occupy until I come!" This is the great commission to stay busy preaching the gospel of the kingdom (Matthew 28:18-20).

Therefore, until Christ returns, every servant (true worshipper of God) has the commanded responsibility to labor for their master in whatever way the Spirit of God chooses to impart to them their pound (spiritual talent or gift), and in whatever way he wishes for them, by faith, to expressively use it to the glory and honor of God.

Christ declared that "the kingdom of heaven suffereth violence, and the violent take it by force" (Matthew 11:12). Through enthusiastic vital activity, then, the Bride of Christ (the church), during her husband's absence, is to be spiritually energetic in always coercing and persuading (pushing and pressing) others into eagerly believing and accepting the gospel message of Jesus Christ. Thereby is ever the multiplying and advancing of the citizenship and dominion of His kingdom within the converted hearts and minds of many of God's repentant sons and daughters.

Until Christ returns, this is our mandated work. When we faithfully do it, we stay ever alert. We stay watchful. We stay ever mindful of our redeemed responsibilities as being appreciative servants of the Lord of the Harvest. It is a for sure safeguard, against having our Lord steal upon us like a thief in the night.

We're neither to be idle talkers nor idly standing around the harvest doing nothing. Our Lord is near to come and blessed will be all those who are found working when He does (Matthew 24:45-51). Those who refuse or just fail to work in the Lord's harvest are said to be asleep in God's eyes; and we must not to be found in such an inactive state when He returns.

The apostle Paul reminds us that we are not of those who are of the night (those in a state of moral darkness and spiritual inactivity) but that we are all children of light. Therefore, we must not be found asleep, but watching and being sober (Thessalonians 5:4–6).

So, as the virgin Bride of Christ, then by obediently laboring unto the coming of the Lord, we will have faithfully proven that We were

Actively **W**aiting **O**ur **K**ing **E**ternal !

Acronym Sixteen

And there was war in heaven; Michael and his angels fought against the dragon and the dragon fought against his angels. (Revelation 12:7)

This cosmic war between the forces of good and evil started when Lucifer, the former Light Bearer of God, grew discontent in his job position as the "anointed cherub that covereth" (Ezekiel 28:14). The particular divine duties of the covering cherub consisted of Lucifer being God's most personal Angelic attendant. Whatever God needed done, Lucifer performed it; he had it covered.

It was Lucifer's honored and privileged duty to also "walk up and down within the midst of the stones of fire" where, on the crystal-clear sapphire terrace of the Most-High, he would direct the endless flow of angelic traffic that would be returning from their untiring flights from innumerable worlds afar, having been sent out on some mission of love from the Eternal Father of Spirits and Lights.

Lucifer was said to be "even wiser than Daniel, and there was no hidden secret of creativity or knowledge that the Triune Godhead could ever hope to hide from him" (Ezekiel 28:3). He was also the most beautifully bejeweled and decorated angel in all of heaven. He was masterfully crafted for maximum eye-effect by the ingenious hand of his Creator.

Even whenever he would open his mouth to speak, beautiful and melodious sounds of all kinds of musical drums and tambourines would be heard! When God first created the world, and fastened together its foundations, and laid the cornerstone thereof, it was Lucifer who led the morning stars in their angelic songs and then orchestratively signaled to the sons of God to gloriously shout for supreme joy! (Job 38:4–7).

Yes, he had it all. He was the wisest, the most beautiful, the most powerful, the most talented, and the brightest. He was perfect from the day that God created him until iniquity was found in him (Ezekiel 28:15). So, despite possessing all of these gifts, Lucifer was not content; he wanted more. He wanted to be like God (Isaiah 14:14); he wanted to sit in the seat of God, showing himself to be God (II Thessalonians 2:4). Although he was but a created servant and not God, he set his heart as the heart of God (Ezekiel 28:1–2).

The Bible sums it all up by saying, "His heart was lifted up because of his beauty, and he corrupted his wisdom by reason of his brightness" (Ezekiel 28:17). Because God would deny Lucifer such a presumptuous and prideful request to "sit upon His throne," Lucifer, with the "tale of his lies" that he would tell about God, had managed to deceive one third of heaven's angels, winning them over to his side (Revelation 12:4).

With this innumerable company of disgruntled and deceived angels, he led an angelic rebellion against God and His government, with the aggravated hopes of forcefully removing God from His Mighty and Majestic throne.

Thus, there was great violence

When **A**ngels **R**ebelled

in heaven!

Acronym Seventeen

For, as by one man's disobedience, many were made sinners. (Romans 5:19)

After Lucifer's expulsion from heaven, the Bible says that Lucifer, now styled the devil and Satan, was cast down to earth, and his angels were cast down with him (Revelation 12:8).

Battlefield earth was to be the next theater of Satan's operations in his declared and continued warfare against God that he and his angels started, yet prevailed not to win in heaven. That's because, before he was expelled, he argued that mankind, in the authoritative-head of Adam, would freely abdicate its earthly kingdom and throne, along with its inherited title, "the god [ruler] of the earth," if another offer of some kind were to come along that he felt would be much better and more deserving to him than the present one that God had already given to him and entrusted him with.

Therefore, it was decided by heaven's high court that such a test of mankind's loyalty towards its Creator should be enacted. This particular test was to come in the form of two trees within the Garden of Eden: the tree of life, and the tree of the knowledge of good and evil.

When God first informed Adam regarding the particular trees from which he could eat and those from which he could not, God was revealing or rather making known to Adam at that very moment his law! The Law of God as Adam then knew and understood it was the "voice of God's free-will" and the "voice of God's restraint"—that which Adam could do and that which he was forbidden from doing. Adam, being created a free-moral agent, would have to decide when the time of his great testing came, as to what he would choose to do—Obey? Or Disobey?

And so, the biblical story sadly goes:

And when the woman saw that the tree was good for food, and it was pleasant to the eyes, and a tree to be desired to make one [self] wise; then she took of the fruit, and did eat, and gave also unto her husband with her; and he did eat. And the eyes of them both were opened, and they knew that they were naked; and they sewed fig leaves together, and made themselves aprons" (Genesis 3:6–7).

At the very moment when Adam hearkened unto the voice of his wife, Eve, above the voice of God, he not only proved by his disobedient actions that he loved Eve more than he loved God, but also, the pointed argument that Satan would later make in the case of Job, which was "bone for bone and flesh for flesh, yea all that a man hath will he give for his life" (Job 2:4). Eve was Adam's very life, his very bone, flesh and skin. Therefore, her very life Satan had placed in dire jeopardy of death!

Making Adam feel that if he couldn't save her, he would be willing to give up everything for the sake of the love that he had for her was Satan's sole strategy. This is what he was diabolically banking on, and it worked!

In any case, the Apostle Paul says that Adam was not deceived, but knowingly and willingly gave up the world for the love of Eve; this free choice left them both naked and exposed to the shameful conflict of sin.

Now, with the Holy Spirit having immediately removed the light of God's righteousness, which was their covering, the spirit of Satan's rebellion entered them in its place. Therefore, within their fleshly nature and spirit, sin took up hostile arms against God. Mankind, in the authoritative form of Adam, sided with the arch-deceiver.

So, this was what happened

When **A**dam **R**ebelled

on earth!

Acronym Eighteen

H.O.M.E.

"In my Father's house are many mansions; if it were not so, I would have told you. I go to prepare a place for you. And if I go and prepare a place for you, I will come again, and receive you unto myself, that where I am, there you may be also." (John 14:2–3)

These particular mansions that Christ went away to prepare for us in heaven are not the type of mansions that we here on earth are accustomed to seeing and staying in. These mansions are rooms or apartments inside the very spacious and unimaginably large residential palace of God the Father.

These rooms, mansion-sized according to heaven's standards, are for the innumerable guests, royal dignitaries and rulers of the sinless, unfallen worlds, who from time to time visit heaven in order to "annually present themselves" before the Lord of all Glory (Job 1:6–7).

These mansion-sized rooms are for friends, family and representatives of the King while they are visiting heaven. And while they are there, God wants their temporary stay to be as pleasing, comfortable, delightful and memorable as possible.

Whatever the decorative case or accommodation may be regarding these particular rooms, they are specifically tailor-made to the individual liking of each ruling representative. The King spares no expense in making sure that His honored guests are well taken care of while they are visiting Him.

When Christ said that He was going to prepare these rooms for us, He meant that He was going away to His Father in order to make a legal argument that those whom He had given Him should be allowed, just like the other visiting dignitaries of the other worlds, to visit heaven in order to behold Him within His Ruling Glory.

This particular prayer of Jesus to His Father was based on the fact that Jesus had begun to anticipate His forthcoming victory over Satan at Calvary. He saw "Satan falling like lightning from heaven" as the "accuser of heaven's brethren" (Revelation 12:10), and He victoriously ascended into heaven in order to take his place as the Rightful Ruler and Representative of this world, thus restoring and giving back to Adam and his righteous descendants through Christ, the first dominion that was lost way back in Eden.

So now, being no longer enemies of God but "friends and guests of the Bridegroom" [Christ] (John 15:15), we have an eternal legal and residential right through Christ (the second Adam) to take up residence in heaven within these rooms for one thousand years, and we'll be living and reigning as kings and priests, both of God and Christ (Revelation 20:4–6).

The Bible says that the heaven of heavens belongs to the Lord, but the earth has He given to the children of men (Psalm 115:16). So heaven is not intended to be our permanent home, but rather a home away from home [the newly created earth]. We will have a home or house that is made, prepared in the heavens by Christ, and we will have a house here on earth that we will build and make with our own hands (Isaiah 65:17–25). I'm very sure that you will have the ability and creativity to make it even better than the one in the heavens if you wish. This is God's eternal gift to you.

So, whether you're there in heaven on business or on vacationing pleasure, then always know that you'll have an eternal:

House Of Magnificent Excellence

in which to reside!

HOPE TO SEE YOU ALL THERE—

MARANATHA!

Acronym Nineteen

Are you waiting to experience that blessed hope,
That aspiring joy we will share
When the trumpet will sound aloud
And the saints will awake to meet the Lord in the air?

Are you waiting for the Lord to appear
With glorious crown in His hand,
When His reward will go forth from before Him
Whether good or bad, to righteously impart to every man?

Are you waiting to see the Lord
Whose face and garments will gleam brighter than the sun;
Whose oceanic voice will proudly say unto you,
"Thou good and faithful servant, well done!"?

Are you waiting for the Lord to change you
In a bright moment in the twinkling of an eye,
When we all will journey beyond Orion's glory,
To that far away place in the sky?

Now, if we expect to experience all of these things, and
By faith into the Lord's coming embrace, we desire to arise;
Then until He appears the second time,
We must continue to

Have Our Patience Exercised!

For in this hope we were saved. Now hope that is seen is not hope. For who hopes for what he sees? But if we hope for what we do not see, we await for it with patience. (Romans 8:24–25)

Acronym Twenty

If you ever get to a point in your life
Where you feel you can't go on,
And you just don't know what else you can do,
Have patience 'til the glorious coming of that blessed hope,
When out from the clouds will appear:

Angels
Singing and rejoicing
with

Jehovah **O**ver **Y**ou!

The Lord your God is in your midst,
a mighty one who will save;
he will rejoice over you with gladness;
he will quiet you by his love;
he will exult over you with loud singing.
(Zephaniah 3:17)

ACRONYM TWENTY-ONE

And he shall speak great words against the most High, and shall wear out the saints of the most High, and think to change times and laws: and they shall be given into his hand until a time and times and the dividing of time. (Daniel 7:25)

Yea, he magnified himself even to the prince of the host, and by him the daily sacrifice was taken away, and the place of his sanctuary was cast down. And an host was given him against the daily sacrifice by reason of transgression, and it cast down the truth to the ground; and it practiced, and prospered....And in the latter time of their kingdom, when the transgressors are come to the full, a king of fierce countenance, and understanding dark sentences, shall stand up. And his power shall be mighty, but not by his own power: and he shall destroy wonderfully, and shall prosper, and practice, and shall destroy the mighty and the holy people. And through his policy also he shall cause craft to prosper in his hand; and he shall magnify himself in his heart, and by peace shall destroy many: he shall also stand up against the Prince of princes; but he shall be broken without hand. (Daniel 8:11–12, 23–25)

And the king shall do according to his will; and he shall exalt himself, and magnify himself above every god, and shall speak marvelous things against the God of gods, and shall prosper till the indignation be accomplished: for that which is determined shall be done. Neither shall he regard the God of his fathers, nor the desire of women, nor regard any god: for he shall magnify himself above all. (Daniel 11:36–37)

Let no man deceive you by any means: for that day shall not come, except there come a falling away first, and that man of sin be revealed, the son of perdition; Who opposeth and exalteth himself above all that is called God, or that is worshipped; so that he as God sitteth in the temple of God, shewing himself that he is God. (II Thessalonians 2:3–4)

<•>

I AM the Universal Shepherd who pastors the flock.
With my crosier-staff, I guide them along the way.
I AM the Prince of the Apostles.
I AM even the Vicarious Filii Dei!

I AM the Sole Interpreter of the Word of God.
On matters of faith and morals,
I will never speak or teach 'ex cathedra' flaws.
I have the keys to heaven and earth.
I AM even He who changed Calendar Times
And divine Sabbath Laws!

My authority is anciently renowned.
I AM earth's last absolute king.
Ten thousand times ten thousand marvel before me.
Even Heads of States do reverently kiss
My gold Fisherman's Ring!

I AM the Mediatory Bridge between God and Man.
I AM the Pontifex Maximus, Latin for "Supreme High-Priest."
I daily sacrifice CHRIST, and of His flesh and blood;
I bid one billion souls, "Drink and eat!"

I AM all these things and so much more.
So listen to these last things that I dogmatically declare:
I AM the One Holy Catholic Apostolic Papa,
The Ecclesiastical Roman

Power **O**ver **P**eople **E**verywhere!

Proverbial Quotations

"Pleasant words are as a honey-comb,
sweet to the soul, and health to the bones."
Proverbs 16:24

Twenty-four Proverbial Quotes

Proverbs

"Adam gave up the world for the love of Eve.
But God gave up His son for the love of the world!"

"Concerning the origin of the universe: faith, logic and reason, righteously affirms a Creator. Evolution, scientific philosophies, big bang theories, and monkey notions only foolishly affirm dogmatic myth."

"The Creationists and Evolutionists all agree on the big bang. The Evolutionist teaches that the world began with one; the Creationist preaches that the world will end with one!"

"Greek myth states that Atlas carried the world upon his shoulders. The Bible says that in the bearing of the cross, Christ carried a much heavier burden on His back. Now, that's a historical fact!"

"To ponder a mystery is to knock on wisdom's door. And only in your persistent patience in trying to solve it will she finally open up to give you the treasure of her reply!"

"True friends are like granite mountains; they are fast-settled by the hand of God and are endurable throughout all times."

"A person who has at least one true friend is both wise and immeasurably rich. A person who has many must ponder them, until fate and adversity try their worth."

"If you are lost and wish to know the way to heaven, then just turn right and stay straight."

"In heaven's blessed estimation, the smallest act of kindness is the greatest act of kindness."

"As the yawning of the mouth proceeds the sleep of a tired soul, then so too does idleness proceed the thought of every evil work."

"A perfect God is coming back for a perfect people at the perfect time and on the perfect day."

"Faith is what a supernatural God gives as supernatural powers unto ordinary people in order for them to accomplish for Him supernatural and extraordinary things."

"As the grinding wheels of an industrial machine continuously put out an ideal product, so do the mental wheels of a studious mind continuously put out a positive and prosperous conduct."

"Through the visions of the eyes, a person's thoughts are vividly painted. But the curatorial eyes of the Lord God survey their eternal worth."

"Morality is the well-tailored garment of righteousness that a nation wears. Immorality, on the other hand, is the loose string of shame that will sinfully unravel it."

"While most Christians are eagerly awaiting the coming of Christ in a cloud, very few realize that before He does, Satan, in all his deceiving glory, will come down upon the same."

"We are saved by grace, so that by faith we might work righteousness by our love for God and Christ in the blessed hopes of one day living and reigning forever with them!"

"The beauty of a woman's face is like that of a painted picture and the stateliness of her body its well-created frame."

"A poor man once told a Christian who attempted to preach to him the risen Christ, "Feed and clothe me first, and when I'm warm and full from your kindness, then I will better perceive the words of your intended sermon."

"In seeking to accomplish His divine will, God always seeks to greatly do, not by many but by one or a few."

"When the scattered clouds of God's bickering people begin to unifiably drift together and become moisturized with truth and righteousness, and their hearts become heavy with the obligatory burden of proclaiming the three-Angels message to the world, then and only then will the heavens begin to pour down promised, blessed rain. Then, a wonderful harvest of lost souls will be instantly brought into the kingdom of Heaven. Oh, to God and Christ, that such an end-time process would begin NOW!"

"The eyes of God's providence peer around the corner of tomorrow in order to supply our needs for today."

"In performing our God-given duties in this life, heaven allots us but a few precious minutes. Oh, how eternally imperative it is, we spend it wisely."

"As Christians, people ought not see the old you, for the sake of Christ who obscures the view."

"If God appoints it, He anoints it. If it has been blessed, you will have success."

"By faith, we knock at the door of the supernatural where heavenly impossibilities become earthly realities."

"There are only four persons who are to be privy to our charities: the person who gives it, the person who receives it, the angel who records it, and God who's pleased with it."

<=>

"When Christians are on fire for God, people gather around to see what's burning!"
—Lewis Hardin

"When Christ comes back the second time, He's not coming as a quiet lamb from Bethlehem, but as a roaring lion from Mount Zion."
—Anthony L. Webb

"The first death is because of the nature of sin. The second death is because of the wages of sin."
—Demetrius Walton

"Struggles are the cost of transforming dreams into reality."
—Lewis Hardin

Poetry Selections

The LORD is my strength and my shield;
My heart trusted in him, and I am helped:
Therefore my heart greatly rejoiceth;
And with my song will I praise him.
Psalm 28:7

Eight Poems by H. Sweet
Three Poems by Others

Sunsets

We daily view such serene sunsets,
Each so beautiful yet never the same.
That's because God's painting for you a 'brand-new day'
In a different picture of a fiery frame.

So next time that you happen to see a sunset,
Learn to appreciate God's daily grace as you pass by,
Because it is He who creatively writes His signature
Across the canvas of the evening sky.

Observations

Fiery-red clouds softly gleaming behind cedar green trees,
Below fading blue skies.
Sun quietly descending horizontal-west,
As its golden rays beckon the new day "awake,"
As the glory of the former one brilliantly dies!

Moon begins her eloquent stride
Amidst a sparkling array of reddish-blue stars.
Orion watches in awe of such celestial beauty,
As earthen gales tweetly herald such a waning waltz from afar.

I once again intently wake,
With that of the smiling sun,
Which lets me know that the second half
Of the new day has just begun!

Morning dew mysteriously frozen
On a carpet of emerald-green grass.
Yes, it's just another splendid observation
Of a crystallized ocean from last night's past.

A Man Named Jesus

There was a man named Jesus who died on Calvary.
There was a man named Jesus
Who gave His life for you and me.
And, on the third day, He arose.
Thus now our souls are set free!

Yes, there IS a man named Jesus who lives eternally.
So, won't you get to know Him and set your soul aright?
Because before you realize it,
He will surely come back like a thief in the night!

When All is Finally Said and Done

When all is finally said and done,
My battles will be over, the victory won!
When in final triumph, from my face will shine
The light of Christ's redeeming grace!
He will then tell me,
"My son, well done, you ran a good race!"

When We Cross the River Jordan

When we cross the River Jordan,
Oh what a wonderful day that will be.
All nations, languages, tongues, and peoples
Proudly standing upon the banks of that fiery, glassy sea.

When we cross the River Jordan,
Oh what a wonderful day that will be.
No more death, sickness, sadness, or sorrow;
Just joy, peace, and happiness throughout all eternity.

When we finally cross the River Jordan,
Oh what a wonderful day that will be.
Crowns of glory, beautiful mansions, monthly fruits of life;
Oh my, this is what CHRIST is preparing for you and me.

(Scripture Reading: *Revelation 15:1–4; 21:1–27; 22:1–5*)

That Outstanding Love of Mine

Oh Jesus, my Savior, most sacred, divine,
Thou art the sweet Rose of Sharon,
Most heavenly sublime.

Gently send down upon me
The sweet fragrance of your grace above,
Causing my soul to take the morning wings
Of your eternal love.

Oh yes, Jesus, a true friend and savior in thee do I find;
So I promise you from this day forward,
You'll always be that "Outstanding Love of Mine!"

So friend, if YOU would like to know how to find
This particular Outstanding Love of Mine,
Give up your sins, cleanse your heart and soul,
Then gaze back to Mount Calvary,
And that very Outstanding Love of Mine you will surely see!

God Walks in the Beauty of the Night

God walks in the beauty of the night.
His head is as the most fine gold.
His eyes are like evening candles,
Moonlit beams guild graceful paths by shimmering light.

God walks in the beauty of the night.
His hands and feet are like burnished bronze in the fires.
His belly shines like pure ivory bright,
Overlaid with blue sapphires.

God walks in the beauty of the night,
His overall appearance, altogether lovely,
So divinely bright.

This is my Beloved,
The Chiefest among ten thousand,
Who walks in the eternal beauty of the night.

(Scripture Reading: *Song of Solomon 5:10–16*)

Salvation

Salvation is trusting by faith in God's plan,
Which came in the form of Jesus, that perfect man,
Who at such infinite cost
Redeemed with His own blood, all that Adam had lost!

Thanks

My eyes open, the morning has come.
Praise unto You, another day for your will to be done.

Let your wisdom fall upon me in season due;
Let me speak of your mercy, for those are new.

How can I withhold the blessings You gave?
Shout will I, the way to be saved!
The stars, though my eyes can not behold;
Exist for the mysteries You will unfold.

While some will hear, some will turn away;
But just to have that chance, You have the praise.

Open my eyes even more to see the deep,
Obeying your precepts, your commandments will I keep.

The words on this page can not explain the life You lead.
Only testifying that obedience is like pure air to me.

—Ri'antre Chapman

Choices

Dreams of a man, he's tossing and turning;
Nightmares of his life, a lost soul burning.

So many times, there were whispers in his ear.
Consumed by darkness, he was too deaf to hear.

The passion of our Christ, the forgiveness of our sins;
A brighter tomorrow, where life never ends.

The struggles we face, the choices we make;
Judgment upon us, will decide our fate!

—Marino Bates

Reading the Bible Through

Every year people read the Bible through.
Though a lot of pages are turned and read,
Understandings are few.

They read the word, yet nothing is learned.
I'd rather study one verse,
Till its meaning is discerned.

This book is filled with hidden wealth,
Preserved through ages of time.
Oh, that they might patiently search it,
To discover its treasures divine!

So all ye who desire to dig, then dig real slow.
For like precious gold and silver,
There's much wisdom and knowledge to know.

Here is WISDOM, which is absolutely true!
You'll miss all that God desires for you to find,
When you hurriedly read the Bible through.

—Ri'antre Chapman

A Preview of Volume 2 . . . .

.....In the beginning the Logos said..........

A Preview of Volume 2

In the beginning was the Word, and the Word was with God, and the Word was God.

The same was in the beginning with God. All things were made by him; and without him was not anything made that was made.   John 1:1-3

The Divine Adage which was in the beginning with God, is inarguably declared to be the LOGOS—the Divine Expression and Omnipotent Voice of God.

The Greek word *logos* (Strong's #3056) is used to describe the preexistent nature of Jesus Christ, and of the glory He shared with His heavenly Father before the world began (see John 17:5).

Before the beginning or ever the earth was, Jesus' preexistence was with and alongside God as the eternally enthroned Word of WISDOM!

As being the verbally creative breath of the Almighty, He has always existed and is the loving expression by which God instantaneously brought all things into being.

This is chiefly understood by the Word of Wisdom Himself, who declares:

The Lord possessed me [as His omnipotent voice] from the beginning of His way [from His eternal existence]...

I was brought forth [as a fiery whirlwind, I was lovingly summoned from deep within His bosom]...

I was by Him [as His wise creative counselor and master craftsman] as being one brought up [eternally existing] equally with him...

(Proverbs 8:22-30)

This ancient oration of wisdom could only have ushered forth from the gracious mouth of Christ, whose divine origins have been said of God to have been "from old, from everlasting" (see Micah 5:2).

The Apostle Paul states that "God created all things by Jesus Christ" and that "Jesus Christ is both the power of God and the wisdom of God" (1 Corinthians 1:24; Ephesians 3:9).

The prophet Jeremiah declares that by this same power and wisdom, "God established the world, and stretched out the heavens by his discretion" (Jeremiah 10:12).

David the psalmist says,

By the Word of the Lord were the heavens made, and all the host by the breath of his mouth.

He [the Logos] spoke, and it was done.

He [the Logos] commanded, and it stood fast.

(Psalms 33:6, 9)

And lastly, the writer of Hebrews concludes that God, through His Son Jesus, made the world(s), and upholds all things by the word of His power (Hebrews 1:2-3).

So, by Him were all things created that are in heaven and that are in earth, visible and invisible, whether they be thrones, or dominions, or principalities, or powers: all things were created by the divine power of the spoken...

Language **O**f **G**od's **O**mnipotent **S**on
Jesus

Yes, it was He in the very beginning, who

Spontaneously **A**chieved **I**t's **D**esign!

(See Genesis 1:1-31)

Who Am I?

Who am I? I am the cloudy weight that distills the crystal-blue rains, that impetuously falls from infinite space. I am the unseen wind beneath the wings of fowls, that evenly glides with eloquent grace.

Who am I? I am the fiery adhesive that moltenly binds together the foundations of this earth. I am the one power of fertilization, that stimulates the miracle of every birth.

Who am I? I am the waning light that shines from the moon; I am even the brightness of the sun and stars. I am He who commands the lightnings, that they may run unto Me and say, "Here we are!"

Who am I? I am the eternal circumference above and beneath the world. I am that witty inventor, who amid fire and water, secretly fashions the diamond, sapphire, and precious pearl.

Who am I? I am the mathematical equations, that nightly chart the constellations high above. I am the way that leads to righteousness and judgment, that even death and hell have heard the fame thereof.

I am counsel, and I am understanding. Thus, by Me princes decree justice and kings do righteously reign. Yes, I am the voice that flowed from Solomon's mouth; it was I, by my riches, who got him his renowned fame.

Who am I? I am the divine Keeper of the celestial months. An by my command they spring forth in their seasonal stages. I am He, who since times eternal have been called THE DESIRE OF AGES.

Who am I? You ask. I am WISDOM. So *blessed* is the man and woman who heareth me, watching daily at my gates, waiting patiently by the posts of my door. For whosoever findeth me shall find life eternal, and shall find favor with the Lord!

(Scriptural Reading: Proverbs 8:1-36)

About the Author

Harold L. Sweet is a fifty-year-old Christian inmate who is presently serving eighty-five percent of a twenty-one year prison sentence for second-degree robbery.

He has had a long history of drug abuse, which has quite naturally led him to spend much of his adult life in and out of the California Prison system. Since his 2002 incarceration, he has been constantly battling all his past demons, and by heavens' forgiving grace, he has been allowing God's Spirit to 'conform' him into the likeness and image of Christ.

He is adamant now, more than ever before about striving to live that godly life and about spreading the Word of God. Through the guidance of the Holy Spirit, he was led to yoke-up with a fellow Christian inmate and friend, Mr. Anthony L. Webb, whom he likes to proudly call "a true reformed champion of the truth," and has been able since that time to help teach and lead many other inmates to Christ and to be baptized. This is the continual work that they both do there at the prison on a daily and weekly basis.

About the Author

A Small B.I.B.L.E of Biblical-Acronyms is the second book Harold has authored while being incarcerated. The first is entitled *Bible of Spiritual Poetry*, a wonderful book of spiritually delightful, thought provoking and heart–moving Christian poems.

He says he's not a poet, but his Christian poems are something that the Holy Spirit 'momentarily' gave him one day while in his prison cell. However, these moments of brief poetic expressions have appeared within prison anthology chapbooks. He won first-place in prison creative writing contests, and a few of his works have been published in three separate editions of the Christian magazine, *The Adventist Review*.

In anticipation of his scheduled release in 2020, he's beginning to lay the ground-work for his very own Christian gift company, called Advent-Aware, which is sure to spiritually take the Christian world by creative storm.

Furthermore, his in-house prison ministry, Sweet-Spirit Ministry, will continue, both while he is in prison as well as upon his release, to not only bring the message of the ETERNAL gospel of Jesus Christ to the prisoners, but also to provide and assist them in meeting some of their social and economic needs as they exist within an incarcerated environment.

So, despite all the adversity that Harold L. Sweet has been through, his life seems to still be very promising! And if he continues to further keep his feet upon the beaten path that leads towards heaven's coming kingdom and keeps his eyes on Christ, it is certain that God will yet do great things for him and through him.

Update: Harold thanks the Lord for allowing him to be released from prison as of the publishing of this version of the book. He is now gainfully employed and excited about serving in this ministry in the wider world.

If you have enjoyed reading this book and would like to make comments, you may contact the author:

Email: HLSweetBibleAcronyms@gmail.com

www.ingramcontent.com/pod-product-compliance
Lightning Source LLC
Chambersburg PA
CBHW071409040426
42444CB00009B/2167